100 Questions & Answers About Codependency

by Cynthia Schiebel, MEd, LPC, LCDC, and Darlene Lancer, JD, LMFT

for
dummies®
A Wiley Brand

100 Questions & Answers About Codependency For Dummies®

Published by: **John Wiley & Sons, Inc.**, 111 River Street, Hoboken, NJ 07030-5774, www.wiley.com

For general information on our other products and services, please contact our Customer Care Department within the U.S. at 877-762-2974, outside the U.S. at 317-572-3993, or fax 317-572-4002. For technical support, please visit https://hub.wiley.com/community/support/dummies.

Wiley publishes in a variety of print and electronic formats and by print-on-demand. Some material included with standard print versions of this book may not be included in e-books or in print-on-demand. If this book refers to media that is not included in the version you purchased, you may download this material at http://booksupport.wiley.com. For more information about Wiley products, visit www.wiley.com.

Library of Congress Control Number is available from the publisher.

ISBN 978-1-394-36870-9 (pbk); ISBN 978-1-394-36872-3 (ebk); ISBN 978-1-394-36871-6 (ebk)

Printed and bound by CPI Group (UK) Ltd, Croydon, CR0 4YY

C9781394368709_060126

Contents at a Glance

Table of Contents

Introduction

Codependency is somewhat controversial — it isn't a clinical diagnosis, and you won't find it listed in the *Diagnostic and Statistical Manual of Mental Disorders*, published by the American Psychiatric Association. Instead, it has its roots among those who treat substance use disorders. The term *codependence* is used to describe a pattern of protective behaviors in order to get needs met, maintain connection, and feel safe. We wrote this book to answer common questions about codependency — what causes it, what it looks like, how codependent relationships differ from healthy relationships, and the recovery options available.

About This Book

This book is a reference, which means you don't need to read the chapters in order from beginning to end and you don't have to remember anything — there isn't a test at the end of it.

Within this book, you may note that some web addresses break across two lines of text. If you're reading this book in print and want to visit one of these web pages, simply key in the web address exactly as it's noted in the text, pretending as though the line break doesn't exist. If you're reading this as an e-book, you've got it easy — just click the web address to be taken directly to the web page.

Foolish Assumptions

In writing this book, we made just a couple of assumptions about you, the reader:

» You're in a codependent relationship or know someone who is.

» You have questions, and you want answers.

If those basic assumptions apply to you, you've come to the right place.

Icon Used in This Book

This book uses the following icon in the margins:

When you see the Tip icon, you'll find information that will make your life a little easier, at least when it comes to codependence.

Where to Go from Here

If you aren't sure where to begin, head to the Table of Contents and skim through the questions until you find one that catches your eye. Or, if you have a specific topic in mind, search for it in the Index. Want to know absolutely everything? Turn the page and start in with Part 1.

1

Understanding Codependency

This part explains what codependency is, what causes it, and the signs of codependency. It also covers the consequences of codependency in people's lives and the connection between codependency and addiction.

Chapter 1

Introducing Codependency

You've probably heard the term *codependency*, but you may not be entirely clear what it means or where it originated. If so, you've come to the right chapter. Here, you find out what codependency is, where it was first identified, and how it's diagnosed.

What Is the History of Codependency?

In the 1950s, scholars began exploring unhealthy family systems and family dynamics. But the word *codependence* didn't pop-up until the 1970s, when it was associated with the addiction/recovery field. At that time, *codependence* referred to the spouse or family member who couldn't stop rescuing, controlling, or covering up the addict's behavior.

With time, therapists and writers began noticing these same patterns in relationships that had nothing to do with addiction — including in friendships, in marriages, and even at work. In 1986, the 12-step program Co-Dependents Anonymous (CoDA) started, opening the doors for treatment and help. Today, though the term *codependence* continues to be debated, the definition and treatment of codependence are more fine-tuned and more inclusive of all relationships that may be impacted by codependency.

How Is Codependency Defined?

Codependency is developmental or relational immaturity rooted in early childhood trauma. This trauma is relational. When a child perceives a caregiver's behavior as less than nurturing, the child's sense of self gets tangled up in someone else's — what their caregiver needs, how their caregiver feels, how their caregiver may react or respond. This, in turn, leads to over-caring, chasing closeness, needing attention to feel secure, overcontrolling, people-pleasing, or under-functioning.

TIP

When people refer to codependence, they're really talking about the ways people abandon themselves in order to stay connected to others.

How Is Codependence Different from Healthy Dependence?

In codependency, your sense of self, value, worth, and safety are filtered through how someone else reacts, feels, thinks, or behaves. Codependence is imbalanced — it keeps a person on a seesaw, moving toward or away to get their underlying needs met and to feel seen, heard, or chosen. The relationship often feels one-sided or draining.

Healthy dependence in relationships is *interdependent.* Your self-worth is stable, regardless of other people's thoughts, feelings, or behaviors. Your personal needs are balanced, you make decisions independently, you respect other people's boundaries and they respect yours, and it feels like you and the person you're in a relationship with are equally invested in the relationship. The relationship is energizing.

Can Codependency Occur in Any Type of Relationship?

Codependent behaviors can occur in any type of relationship — between parents and children, between siblings, in friendships, in work settings, and, of course, in romantic relationships. Some people even recognize their codependent behaviors with their pets!

How Is Codependency Diagnosed?

Codependency is not a diagnosable mental health disorder identified in the *Diagnostic and Statistical Manual of Mental Disorders,* the reference book published by the American Psychiatric Association that defines and classifies mental health disorders. However, mental health professionals can assess and identify codependency based on patterns of behavior, emotional symptoms, and relationship dynamics. Clinical interviews, self-assessment questionnaires, and an exploration of family history can help identify and treat codependency.

Chapter **2**

Understanding What Causes Codependency

I f you're struggling with codependency, you may wonder where it came from, how it began, or who's to blame. But understanding codependency isn't about assigning blame — blame doesn't help and rarely leads anywhere useful. What matters is understanding how you learned codependency, because that awareness is what enables you to break the pattern and choose a different path forward. This chapter explains what causes codependency.

How Does Codependency Develop?

The root of codependence is relational trauma, which impacts how a child relates to themselves and to others. Codependency usually grows out of early relationships. If, as a kid, the people you depended on weren't emotionally available — maybe they were distracted, unpredictable, or unavailable for any number of reasons — you learned to adapt to get their attention (for example, by pleasing, achieving, or following the rules). Or, if your caregivers were too intrusive, enmeshing, or shaming (think: helicopter parenting), you learned to build walls or walk on eggshells to keep yourself safe.

When a child's needs are not met in a consistent and healthy way, the child learns that love and safety are conditional. Because the child is smart, they "adapt" to the primary caregiver's behaviors in order to maintain connection and safety — and in order to survive.

These adaptations worked when you were little. They helped you cope, feel secure, and get your needs met. But when these behaviors follow you into adulthood, they shape how you show up with partners, friends, family, and coworkers. And that's when most people discover their codependency — as adaptive, protective behaviors that contribute to relationship challenges.

What Role Does Family History Play in Codependency?

You absorb your family's patterns without even realizing it. If you grew up watching a parent over give, rescue, or abandon themselves for the sake of keeping the peace, that behavior gets wired into you as "normal." If a parent's love was tied to performance — "Be good," "Make me proud," "Don't rock the boat" — you learned to *earn* love instead of just receiving it.

When people experience any of the following as children, they often carry their wounds into adulthood and into their own parenting:

» Having their needs be ignored, minimized, or shamed

» Experiencing boundaries that were rigid or nonexistent

» Having caregivers who were abusive, neglectful, or unavailable

If you experienced any of these issues as a child, you'll *unconsciously* repeat your own survival patterns. These dynamics pass down quietly, generation to generation, until someone names them and starts breaking the cycle. These generational patterns are sometimes referred to as *generational trauma* or *legacy burdens*.

TIP

Understanding these patterns of relating isn't about blame — it's about learning to break a cycle. The goal is to heal your own wounds so you can learn new ways to connect with yourself and with others and pass on new relational skills.

How Do Childhood Experiences Contribute to Codependency?

When you're little, you learn how safe it is to be yourself by how the adults around you respond. If your feelings are ignored, shamed, punished, or dismissed (for example, "Don't be so sensitive," "There's nothing to cry about," "Don't use that tone with me"), you may grow up doubting your own reality. You may learn that expressing your truth is unsafe. You may suppress your emotions or mold yourself into a role that will keep the peace — walking on eggshells, caretaking, achieving, peacemaking, or being invisible.

If love feels conditional (for example, "I'll be proud of you if . . ."), you may learn to perform instead of just *be*. If you're raised in an environment where abuse, neglect, enmeshment, abandonment, or inconsistent caregiving is present, you may learn that survival depends on adapting to the needs and moods of the adults around you. Instead of developing a strong sense of self, you become hyperfocused on reading others, pleasing them, or managing their emotions to avoid rejection, abandonment, or harm (for example, "I will adapt, to keep you connected — because I need you for survival"). In the process, you lose touch with a solid sense of self.

These early survival strategies show up later, in adult relationships, as codependency. These survival strategies helped you to navigate childhood, but they become barriers to intimacy, self-esteem, self-care, and healthy boundaries in adulthood.

How Do Societal and Cultural Factors Influence Codependency?

Culture has a big say in how codependency plays out. In some families or communities, sacrifice is seen as love — especially for women. We're taught to put everyone else first, to nurture, sacrifice, and maintain harmony — even if it means erasing yourself in the process.

In some communities, men are expected to be strong and protective and avoid vulnerability. They learn to over-function as "fixers" or avoid emotion to appear strong. Some cultures prize independence so much that needing others at all feels shameful, pushing people toward rigid boundaries and emotional distance.

Religious or moral teachings may provide messages of self-denial, unquestioning service, and unconditional forgiveness. These teachings may result in tolerating abuse, neglecting self-care, or avoiding boundaries under the guise of "love" or "faith."

In work environments, your value may be measured by productivity, success, or how indispensable you are. These career norms may result in difficulty separating self-worth and value from production, becoming unable to set limits, having difficulty taking a vacation, or having trouble taking care of yourself without guilt.

Society can reinforce codependency by rewarding self-abandonment or punishing vulnerability, and that makes recovery trickier because the culture is often cheering on the very patterns that keep you stuck.

Chapter **3**

Recognizing the Signs of Codependency

Although codependency isn't an official diagnosis, mental health professionals identify it through a consistent set of behavioral and emotional patterns. This chapter walks you through the signs they look for so you can begin to see your own patterns more clearly.

What Are the Characteristics Professionals Look for to Assess Codependency?

Professionals can assess codependency through interviews, assessment tools, and patterns of behavior within relationships — with yourself and with others.

Common signs of codependency include the following:

» Excessive caretaking and people-pleasing

» Difficulty owning your own reality (what *you* think, feel, and prefer versus what *others* want you to think, feel, or prefer)

» Poor boundaries with self and others

» Self-esteem issues (difficulty valuing yourself from within as opposed to valuing yourself only through other people's feedback or responses)

» Difficulty knowing and attending to your personal needs and wants

» Control issues (too much or too little)

» Fear of abandonment or rejection

What Are Some Examples of These Characteristics?

Here are some examples of codependent behaviors:

» **Excessive caretaking and people-pleasing:** Rescuing, prioritizing someone else's needs over your own, canceling your own plans to keep others from being upset

» **Difficulty owning your own reality:** Difficulty knowing what your thoughts or feelings are or not being able to name them or share them; difficulty owning your behavior and its impact on others; difficulty seeing your appearance accurately (for example, being underweight but thinking you're overweight)

» **Poor boundaries:** Having trouble saying "no"; feeling guilty or anxious when you do say "no"; having difficulty separating your feelings from others; getting involved in other people's business without being asked; being walled off, too rigid, or too self-contained

» **Self-esteem issues:** Living through someone else's reactions, defining your self-worth through other people's approval or by your accomplishments, feeling responsible for someone else's emotions or happiness, feeling less than or better than someone else

- » **Control issues:** Trying to manage other people's lives or emotions to feel secure, trying to keep other people's emotional boat steady, trying to "fix" or "rescue" instead of letting others resolve their own issues, covering for someone else's mistakes, creating intensity, expressing extreme emotion, or having "either/or" solutions to problems in order to manipulate others to get them to change
- » **Fear of abandonment or rejection:** Doing anything to keep the relationship, tolerating mistreatment to avoid being alone, avoiding conflict or expressing your own feelings to keep the peace, "walking on eggshells" around someone

What Are the Five Core Symptoms of Codependency?

Pia Mellody (1942–2025), who did groundbreaking work defining and treating codependency, described five core issues present in codependence. These five core issues are a great assessment tool for the presence of codependency:

- » **Self-esteem:** Your sense of self-worth depends on what others think of you or on external reward; you feel less than or better than rather than equal.
- » **Boundaries:** You have difficulty setting functional boundaries; you have too few

boundaries (allowing others' thoughts, words, or behaviors to affect you) or too many boundaries (keeping others out and withdrawing when you need connection).

» **Reality:** You have difficulty knowing and expressing your own reality — what *you* think, feel, need, or want. You may adapt your reality to please others or to avoid conflict.

» **Dependence/self-care:** You may have too little self-care, believing others' needs are more important than your own. You may also believe that asking for help is selfish or unsafe. You have difficulty with *interdependence* (the ability to be mutually reliant and express give and take collaboratively as an act of care between yourself and others).

» **Moderation:** Your emotions, behaviors, or reactions are often extreme — either over-reactive or under-reactive. Moderation and balance in all things is challenging and unfamiliar to you.

How Can I Recognize If I'm in a Codependent Relationship?

Codependent relationships can be recognized by patterns — in yourself and in your relationship with others. You'll notice it in the little ways you disappear.

Maybe you're always scanning the other person's mood or you anticipate a response or reaction before you decide how you feel or think or what to do. Maybe you keep saying "yes" when your body is begging you to say "no." Or maybe you can't relax unless the other person is okay — even if you're falling apart inside.

On one end of the continuum, you may become rigid and controlling, doing everything to keep the relationship safe. On the other end, you may chase after them. Either extreme is a sign that the balance is off and codependency is in the mix. And remember, these relationship patterns can happen in any relationship — with your family, your romantic partner, your children, your coworkers, or your friends.

Here are some additional signs to watch for:

>> **Your self-worth is tied to the relationship.** You feel valuable when you're needed, approved of, or in control. You fear losing your identity if you lose the relationship.

>> **You put others' needs above your own.** You sacrifice your time, energy, money, and health to care for someone else. You rarely ask, "What do I need?" — or you feel guilty when you do.

>> **You feel responsible for other people's emotions.** Their mood dictates your mood. If they're sad, angry, or anxious, you feel it's your job to "fix" them, to steady their boat.

» **Boundaries may appear as too little or too much.** You have difficulty saying "no" without guilt or fear of rejection. You may overshare or be an open book. You tolerate unacceptable behavior to keep the relationship, or you wall off others to feel safe and secure.

» **You avoid conflict at all costs.** Disagreements feel threatening to the relationship.

» **You may feel trapped, but you're afraid of letting go.** You think you can't live without them, or they can't live without you. You stay in relationships out of fear, guilt, or obligation.

» **The relationship feels one-sided, not mutually invested.** You give more than you receive — emotionally, physically, financially, mentally, and spiritually.

Chapter **4**

Identifying the Consequences of Codependency

The effects of codependency are pervasive. It can distort your sense of self, undermine your confidence, and interfere with healthy decision-making. Over time, it can also impact physical and mental health. This chapter explores these consequences, not only so you recognize the toll codependency is taking on your life, but so you understand why healing and building new patterns of thought and behavior are essential.

What Are the Emotional Consequences of Codependency?

The emotional impact of codependency may be difficult to see from the outside. But *inside,* codependency is taking a toll because you're constantly abandoning yourself to stay connected to others. Over time, that leads to feelings of emptiness, resentment, or even anger — though many codependents have a hard time expressing those feelings. Guilt and shame may arise when you say "no" or when you try to prioritize your needs. Fear may arise when you experience the possibility of rejection, disapproval, or not being chosen. There's often an undercurrent of anxiety when trying to "fix" others and resentment when taking responsibility for others' emotions, needs, or problems. You may have the thought, "If I were enough, I wouldn't have to work so hard to keep love."

Pouring so much energy into other people is exhausting. And ironically, the very thing you're trying to avoid — disconnection — ends up happening, because without your true self present, intimacy can't really flourish. The emotional cost of codependency is losing touch with your own worth and authentic self. But with help, recovery can happen and you can reclaim your sense of self.

How Does Codependency Shape a Person's Sense of Identity and Self-Worth?

Codependency makes it difficult to connect with the realization that you have *inherent* value and worth. In codependency, your self-worth depends on what other people think, on external achievements, and on being needed and approved of. You feel "less than" (one down, not enough, worthless) or "better than" (one up, entitled, falsely empowered), rather than equal, important, and worthwhile. Over time, this erodes the internal compass that tells you who *you* are. As you rebuild your inner sense of self, self-worth becomes less about performance and more about being. You begin to realize you have worth, not because of what you do, say, or achieve, but simply because you exist.

How Does Codependency Influence Decision-Making?

Codependency skews the ability to own your own reality — to clearly identify your own thoughts, feelings, and preferences — which makes decisions difficult. You may make decisions too hastily, without much thought, or you may be unable to make a decision at all.

When you're codependent, your decisions are often filtered through the *anticipation* of someone else's response — what the other person may think, say, or do. Therefore, you calculate your decisions to avoid conflict and to minimize the risk of rejection, disapproval, or abandonment.

What Are the Physical Health Implications of Codependency?

When your body and brain experience anxiety, stress, and emotional overwhelm, these emotions have a direct impact on your physical health. You may have reduced immunity to disease, higher blood pressure, poor sleep patterns, poor nutrition, and difficulty taking care of your needs (for example, physical hygiene, medical/dental care, physical nurturing, emotional nurturing, earning, saving, budgeting, and investing).

Because codependency includes people-pleasing and behaviors to avoid conflict, rejection, or abandonment, you may also be at risk of tolerating physical, mental, emotional, and/or sexual abuse.

How Does Codependency Impact Relationships?

No relationship is spared when codependency is present. Family relationships, romantic relationships, friendships, and work relationships are all impacted by codependency. In an effort to feel safe, to create connection, to minimize the risk of rejection, disapproval, and/or abandonment, codependent behaviors such as people-pleasing, "fixing" people, caretaking, and controlling are present in the relationship.

In families, the codependent dance to feel safe and secure may be rewarded with praise for being "a good girl" or "a brave boy." In romantic relationships, partners may lose themselves, putting their own needs on the back burner while trying to please, maintain balance, and avoid any risk of abandonment. In the workplace, staying late, taking on extra projects, and being the office "fixer" often lead to resentment, exhaustion, and burnout.

TIP

The ultimate cost of codependency — in any relationship — is the loss of honest, intimate, and authentic expression of self.

Can Codependency Lead to Other Mental Health Issues?

Codependency doesn't usually travel alone. When you spend years ignoring your own needs and bending yourself into a pretzel to keep other people happy, it can stir up all kinds of mental health struggles. Codependency can lead to anxiety — you may live in a constant state of hypervigilance, always wondering, "Are they upset? Am I safe? Do I matter?" Depression can occur, too, because self-abandonment leaves you feeling empty, hopeless, and/or unseen. Other mental health issues that may occur include obsessive-compulsive disorder, attachment disorders, and substance use disorders.

Codependency itself isn't listed as a mental illness, but the patterns can open the door to other conditions if they go unaddressed. Healing those patterns early can be a kind of prevention — it restores balance before the weight becomes too heavy.

What Are the Long-Term Effects of Codependency?

Over the long haul, codependency wears down both the self and relationships. When you're always bending yourself into a pretzel, over-giving, or walling off, you lose touch with your own identity. Over years, many people wake up and realize they don't even know what they want, who they are, or what makes them feel alive outside of managing their relationships. That loss of self can lead to chronic emptiness, low self-worth, and difficulty trusting.

Relationships also pay the price. Codependent patterns tend to result in burnout, resentment, and disconnection over time. What started as love and care can shift into a sense of obligation and duty, resulting in a narrowing of your life — less freedom, less joy, less authenticity.

Recovery is about widening that space again, so your relationships can be rooted in choice, not compulsion, grounded in respect and compassion, confident in the ability to give and receive love without losing yourself.

Chapter **5**

Looking at the Connection between Codependency and Addiction

C *odependency* as a term has its roots in the addiction treatment community, and for good reason: The two often occur together. This chapter explains the connection between codependency and addiction.

What Is the Connection between Codependency and Addiction?

Every addict has an undercurrent of codependence. Someone struggling with codependency may not have an addiction to a substance, but they do have an addiction to a *way of relating* to get their needs met and to feel safe and connected.

Codependency and addiction often dance together. When someone is using, the codependent person may step in to manage, cover, or rescue — thinking they're helping. In reality, they're propping up, or enabling, the addiction. For the codependent, that rescuing, people-pleasing, caretaking, and controlling can feel like its own kind of addiction — the "drug" is the relationship rather than a substance. Both the addict and the partner dealing with codependency are numbing pain — one through substances, and the other through people.

In families where an addiction is present, children learn to adapt to the addict's behavior in order to get their needs met. This pattern of relating gets wired in and continues into adult relationships, with the codependent person often picking someone familiar to relate with — someone with an addiction or another form of unavailability. And sometimes, the codependent behaviors can develop into substance addictions as a way to escape the pain of unresolved trauma.

How Can Codependent Behaviors Enable Addiction?

Enabling is a process in which a person contributes to the continuation of unhealthy or maladaptive behaviors in another person, often unintentionally. Enabling doesn't mean you support the addict's behaviors. Instead, it reflects how you learned early that your own safety, worth, and sense of connection depend on managing others. You may cover up for the addict, make excuses for the addict's behavior, provide money that supports the addiction, or rescue the addict from crises.

Although these behaviors may look and feel like care, they actually prevent the addict from having to be accountable for their behaviors and from experiencing the natural consequences of their behaviors. The addict remains sick, the family system stays dysfunctional, and the codependent only gets temporary relief from their own anxiety, fear, guilt, or need for control.

What Are the Challenges of Dealing with Codependency and Addiction Simultaneously?

Because both codependency and addiction are rooted in childhood experiences, both serve as survival strategies. It's like trying to untangle two knots at once — the addicted person is caught in the cycle of using, while the codependent person is caught in the cycle of rescuing, controlling, and caretaking. Each person feeds the other. If the addict stumbles, the codependent rushes in to fix, rescue, control, and enable, making it easier for the addiction to continue. And if the codependent starts pulling back, they can feel guilt and fear, or the addict may confront them with "What's wrong? Are you mad at me? You're acting like you don't care about me."

Recovery is complicated because both people need to heal at the same time, but often they're locked in a dance that keeps them circling the same pain. Both people are using — either substances or processes — to deal with pain, fear, or shame as a result of childhood wounds. Breaking this cycle requires both partners to get help. They must both develop a tolerance to the discomfort of withdrawal and the skill to learn to live from a place of truth and balance rather than fear.

Can Codependent Behavior Trigger Addictive Tendencies?

When someone is living in a codependent pattern — rescuing, people-pleasing, controlling, abandoning themselves — they often feel empty, resentful, or invisible. That pain can become an activator for addiction — a way to numb the pain. For the addict, they may feel suffocated by control, being criticized, or monitored. These conditions can heighten shame in the addict — and shame is one of the most powerful activators for addictive behavior.

Codependency doesn't *cause* addiction, but it can create the emotional storm that makes addictive behaviors a great escape. Breaking this cycle requires recovery on both sides: The codependent needs to learn balance — support without enabling, care without control — and the addict needs to learn to tolerate reality without resorting to substances. *Both* partners need to learn boundaries, reclaim self-esteem, heal childhood wounds, and actively engage in self-care.

What Are the Signs of Codependency in a Relationship with an Addict?

The signs of codependency (see Chapter 2) look similar in a relationship with an addict. You'll notice yourself behaving more like a manager than a partner. You'll find yourself covering up their mistakes, smoothing over their messes, lying for them to save face with others. You're riding the rollercoaster of their highs and lows, and your own sense of peace is tied to whether they're sober or using. You try to anticipate the addict's responses to your thoughts, words, feelings, and behaviors, and you adjust or filter to avoid conflict, disapproval, rejection, and abandonment. Your own thoughts, feelings, or needs are put on a back burner, while the addict's needs are right up front.

Instead of a relationship between two adults, the relationship starts looking like a parent–child relationship. You may notice yourself thinking, "Are they okay? What do I need to do to keep things from falling apart?" These thoughts are red flags that codependency is at play. Ultimately, instead of living from your truth, you find yourself living in reaction to the addict's illness.

Can Overcoming Codependency Aid in Addiction Recovery?

When a codependent person starts detaching within the relationship — setting boundaries, letting consequences play out, speaking truthfully, honoring their own reality — they stop fueling the cycle. That shift creates space for the addicted person to be accountable and face their own behaviors. It's not easy — the pull to rescue is strong — but every time a codependent person honors their own needs and contains the urge to manage someone else's needs, they model real recovery. That courage can ripple outward, supporting the addict's journey, too.

For the addict, their journey means not only addressing their substance or process addiction, but also addressing their own codependent patterns. Many addicts use substances because they never learned how to tolerate feelings of shame, loneliness, or self-care in healthy ways. As they recover, they also learn the skills of healthy self-esteem, boundaries, and self-care — the very foundations of codependence recovery. Healing codependence not only supports the family system, but also strengthens the addict's capacity to live sober, connected, and free.

What Are Some Additional Examples of How Healing Codependency Impacts Addiction Recovery?

Here are some examples of how codependency impacts addiction recovery:

» When the codependent sets healthy boundaries, the addict faces natural consequences that can motivate change and responsibility for their behaviors.

» When the codependent reclaims self-esteem and personal worth, the addict is free from being someone else's project.

» When the codependent tolerates discomfort without control, the addict can learn emotional regulation and to live without numbing.

» When the codependent speaks truth instead of hiding or covering up, the addict is allowed honesty to become the foundation for lasting sobriety.

>> When the codependent reparents their wounded inner child, the codependent models healing the original wounds that drive the codependency dance.

How Can I Provide Healthy Support for an Addicted Loved One?

When you love someone who's struggling with addiction, the temptation is to rescue — to believe if you just love them enough, they'll get better. But here's the hard truth: over-helping, over-controlling, or over-sacrificing can keep everyone stuck. Healthy support looks like stepping back, letting natural consequences happen, and caring for yourself in the process. True support requires balance — loving the person while refusing to enable the disease, standing in truth rather than in rescue.

Here are some examples of codependent support versus healthy support:

Codependent Support	Healthy Support
Avoids setting boundaries out of fear of abandonment	Sets clear, consistent boundaries with respect and compassion
Rescues the addict from consequences	Allows the addict the dignity to experience the natural outcomes of their choices
Feels responsible for the addict's recovery	Recognizes that the addict's recovery is their responsibility

Codependent Support	Healthy Support
Confuses love with controlling or rescuing	Understands that love is truth, respect, and boundaries
Believes that if they try harder, the addict will change	Believes that if they keep trying, *they* will change — and the addict is responsible for their own change, too

What Are the Treatment Options for Codependency and Addiction?

Treatment for codependency and addiction requires addressing both the individual wounds and the relational patterns that keep the dance in motion. For the addicted person, that may mean detox, rehab, a 12-step program, and/or individual therapy. For the codependent, it may mean intensive treatment, a 12-step program like Al-Anon or Co-Dependents Anonymous (CoDA), and/or individual counseling. Sometimes couples therapy or family therapy helps everyone to see the patterns they've been locked in.

TIP

Healing happens when each person takes responsibility for their own recovery instead of trying to fix the other person, addressing their individual wounds and their relational patterns. It's two people standing on their own feet — *choosing* to be in a relationship from a place of truth and love rather than *having* to be in a relationship for survival.

What Role Do Self-Help Groups Play in Addressing Codependency and Addiction?

Self-help groups play a crucial role in addressing both codependency and addiction. Groups like Al-Anon, CoDA, Alcoholics Anonymous (AA), and other 12-step programs are powerful because they break isolation. When you walk into a room and hear your own story come out of someone else's mouth, the shame starts to lift. You realize you aren't alone and your experience is not unique to you.

Self-help groups also teach tools — like how to detach with love, or how to set boundaries without guilt — and offer connection without judgment. Both the addict and the codependent need community, because recovery isn't something we can muscle through by ourselves — it happens in connection and community. Realizing you aren't alone can be profoundly healing if you grew up feeling unseen, unheard, or responsible for everyone else's well-being.

2

Codependency in Relationships and Culture

Although many people think of romantic relationships when they think of codependency, it can occur in any kind of close relationship. This part looks at how codependency can play out in families, romantic relationships, friendships, and other relationships (for example, at work or with caregivers). It also explores how codependency is treated in culture and media — everything from TV and movies to social media and more.

Chapter **6**

Codependency in Families

Codependency is rooted in families — your family is where you learned to be codependent. And you may continue that codependent pattern with your family of origin (with your parents or siblings) or in your family as an adult (with your partner or children). This chapter explains how codependency looks in families, including how it affects parenting.

How Does Codependency Differ in Familial Relationships?

In familial relationships, codependency often takes on a unique intensity, because roles are rooted in early attachment and identity. Children may adopt roles such as caretaker, fixer, and achiever to feel safe and to keep the family system balanced. They may learn to ignore their own needs to keep the peace, or to over-function so things don't fall apart.

These patterns are wired in and become the blueprint for relating. Unlike friendships or romantic partnerships, you can't just walk away from family as a kid, so you adapt. That's why codependency in families can feel so deeply ingrained — it's the soil you grew up in.

What Is the Role of Codependency in Parent–Child Relationships?

When codependency shows up between a parent and a child, the roles are often reversed. Instead of the parent meeting the child's needs and doing the emotional "heavy lifting" in the relationship, it's the child doing the "heavy lifting" to meet the parent's emotional needs. For example, a parent may go to their child for emotional support after fighting with their spouse, or a parent may expect their child to be "the responsible one" who manages household chaos. This blurring of parent–child positions (called *parentification*) robs the child of a normal, age-appropriate developmental experience.

When this experience and the adapted behaviors follow the child into adulthood, the results are struggling with boundaries, feeling overly responsible for others' emotional state of being, and engaging in relationships where rescuing feels like love.

How Does Codependency Impact Parenting?

A healthy parent provides affirmation, nurturance, and limits while allowing the child to develop a sense of autonomy. A codependent parent may be critical or neglectful; have poor boundaries; or rely on the child for comfort, approval, or even identity — blurring the line between adult and child. They may be too involved with the child, leading to enmeshment, or they may be under-involved, leading to fears of abandonment and anxious attempts to be seen and heard.

These inconsistencies teach a child to adapt to their parent's needs instead of connecting to their authentic self. The child feels responsible for the parent's emotional state of being, or walks on eggshells, always attuned to the parent's needs instead of connecting to their own.

What Are Some Examples of Codependent Parenting Behaviors?

Codependent parenting behaviors include the following:

» **Rescuing:** Never letting a child fail or struggle — doing the child's homework, intervening in conflicts, or shielding the child from natural consequences of their behavior. Though it may look like love, rescuing prevents the child from building resilience, learning responsibility, and building confidence in their own abilities.

» **Guilting or shaming:** Using guilt and/or shame to control the child's choices (for example, saying, "How could you act this way after all I do for you?"). Guilting or shaming teaches the child that their value and worth is tied to pleasing others and that love must be earned.

» **Over-identification:** Pushing the child into certain activities to fulfill your unmet dreams or placing expectations on a child's success to calm your own fears of failure. This behavior robs the child of individuality and creates pressure to *do* instead of simply *be*.

- » **Fear-based control:** Micromanaging every detail of the child's life (as in helicopter parenting) — who they spend time with, how they dress, or what career they pursue. This communicates to the child that they aren't capable of handling life on their own and that they're responsible for making you feel okay.
- » **Emotional invalidation:** Minimizing or dismissing the feelings a child expresses (for example, saying, "There's nothing to be sad about" or "You shouldn't be angry"). The child learns to distrust their own emotions, perhaps becoming unable to identify their feelings or express them in a healthy way.

TIP

Healthy parenting shifts from using the child to meet the parent's needs, to empowering the child to know their own self-worth, to be independent, and to use their voice.

Is It Possible for Codependency to Exist in Sibling Relationships?

Codependent behaviors develop in response to an innate need to survive within the family system. Siblings may form enmeshed bonds — avoiding disagreements, keeping secrets, or sacrificing individuality for the "good" of the family. If one sibling struggles with addiction or destructive behavior, another may become the "hero," cleaning up the sibling's messes or striving for perfection to distract from their behavior. In other situations, a sibling may be assigned the role of "caretaker" of their brothers and/or sisters (essentially coparenting) while putting their own needs on a back burner. These experiences lock siblings in roles instead of allowing them to develop authentic, separate identities.

Chapter **7**

Codependency in Romantic Relationships

R omantic relationships may be what you think of when you think of codependency — and that makes sense, because codependency, which is rooted in childhood, often shows up in the most significant relationships we have as adults. This chapter walks you through how codependency occurs in romantic relationships and how it affects them.

How Does Codependency Manifest in Romantic Relationships?

In romantic relationships, codependency often shows up as an imbalance of energy — one partner over-functioning while the other is under-functioning.

The over-functioning partner is doing the emotional heavy lifting, over-giving, trying to manage their partner's moods, or making themselves small so their partner won't leave. These behaviors are usually fueled by a fear of abandonment and the need to keep a connection at all cost.

The under-functioning partner may feel smothered, infantilized, or overly needed for the well-being of their partner. A fear of intimacy or being seen may fuel reactions of withdrawal, defensiveness, or acting out, while at the same time, they may feel a sense of obligation to remain connected to the relationship.

The codependent cycle starts to feel lopsided — based on survival instead of freedom. Partners stay in relationships out of fear, rather than freedom, love, and intimacy.

What Are Some Signs of Codependency in a Romantic Relationship?

All the characteristics of codependency are present in romantic relationships, with the focus of attention being on the partner:

» **People-pleasing:** Sacrificing your own needs, preferences, or values to keep the relationship steady; saying "yes" when you want to say "no"; fearing rejection or conflict if you rock the boat

» **Poor boundaries (too few or too many):** Feeling responsible for your partner's emotions; taking on their anger, sadness, or anxiety as if it were your own; walling off or being too contained; being afraid to share your true thoughts or feelings because you fear rejection, disapproval, and/or abandonment

» **Jealousy and control:** Attempting to monitor or control your partner's friendships, activities, or choices because you believe this will prevent rejection, betrayal, or abandonment

» **Emotional ups and downs:** Feeling like the relationship is all-consuming, chaotic, draining, and unpredictable

These behaviors are adapted behaviors rooted in early childhood experiences. People often project onto their adult relationships the expectation that *this* relationship will "right" their original, primary relationships with their parents or other caregivers.

How Can Codependency Affect Marriage?

In marriage, codependency can quietly erode intimacy, trust, and mutual investment. When codependency is present, one or both partners lose their individuality and begin functioning in roles — for example, rescuer and dependent, or controller and pleaser. Decisions are made out of fear rather than out of honesty. Resentment builds, with one person carrying too much, while the other avoids responsibility. This cycle erodes trust and creates emotional distance, even if the couple remains legally or physically together. And if addiction or other destructive behaviors are part of the marriage, codependency can lock the couple in a cycle of enabling. The codependent's attempts to manage or rescue often keep the destructive behavior alive, while the addict's dysfunction validates the caretaker's role.

The spark of true partnership dims when the marriage becomes about survival, managing, or caretaking, instead of mutual respect and shared growth.

TIP

In a healthy union, both individuals bring their full, authentic selves into the relationship, taking responsibility for their own feelings and behaviors. Partners are mutually invested.

How Do I Talk with My Partner about Codependency?

Talking to your partner about codependency requires courage, honesty, and compassion. Talking about it can stir up fear, shame, or defensiveness. Start with your own experience, not an accusation. Instead of saying, "You're so codependent," try saying:

> I've noticed I sometimes lose myself in trying to keep you happy, and I don't want that to hurt our relationship.

Or

> I've been learning about codependency, and I recognize some of these patterns in myself. I'd like to work on being healthier in our relationship, and I'd love for us to explore this together.

By owning your part, you reduce blame and create safety for your partner to listen. Codependency is tender territory, so compassion is key.

Frame it as something you'd like to learn about *together*. Invite curiosity. Maybe suggest reading a book or listening to a podcast together. Share what you're hopeful for in the relationship — open communication, clear boundaries, shared responsibility, and deeper intimacy. For example, you might say:

> I want us to feel free to be ourselves, without fear of losing each other. I want us to experience mutual investment, to share freely without fear of rejection, and have each other's back no matter what.

Finally, be prepared to set boundaries with love and respect. If your partner resists or becomes defensive, remind yourself that you can't control their reaction — you can only share your truth with respect and compassion. Offer resources, but respect your partner's choice to engage or not. True recovery from codependency begins when you honor your *own* needs and feelings, regardless of how the other responds.

Chapter **8**

Codependency in Friendships and Other Relationships

When you grow up in an environment that fosters codependency, it may show up in the places you least expect as an adult. For example, you may find yourself in a codependent relationship with a friend or with your boss. This chapter tackles these other ways in which codependency can make itself known.

What Are Signs of a Codependent Friendship?

In friendships, codependency tips the balance away from mutual investment. One person feels they're doing all the giving, while the other is doing all the taking. One friend may be the one dropping everything to help, but when they need support, the other friend is nowhere to be found. Or, one friend is doing the emotional adjusting to keep the other friend's emotional boat steady.

Perhaps there's an emotional drain in the friendship — instead of leaving you energized and connected, the friendship leaves you feeling drained, guilty, or resentful . . . yet you feel guilty and unable to walk away. Jealousy or possessiveness may be present, too — a codependent friend may feel threatened when you spend time with others or expect exclusivity in your loyalty.

Healthy friendships are mutual, with a balance of give and take, respect and compassion.

TIP

Can Codependency Affect Professional Relationships?

In the workplace, the same core issues — poor boundaries, people-pleasing, over-responsibility, over-functioning, fear of rejection — can show up with colleagues, a team, or a boss. When codependent patterns continue, over time, resentment builds, and work becomes less about contributing and more about proving your value. The professional relationship becomes based on fear, compliance, image, and control rather than mutual respect, shared agreements, and clear boundaries.

What Are Some Examples of Codependency in a Workplace Setting?

With your boss or supervisor, you may take on extra projects because you don't want to disappoint; you may stay late or arrive early so no one judges you for not being a team player; or you may feel guilty taking time off, because you don't want to be viewed as unhelpful or not pulling your weight.

You may cover for colleagues, picking up tasks that aren't yours to protect them. You may avoid giving them honest feedback for fear it will upset them.

As a manager or supervisor, you may micromanage your team members' work because you feel their mistakes reflect on you, or you may rescue struggling employees by doing their work for them instead of holding them accountable and allowing them to grow. You may avoid difficult conversations about boundaries or performance because you fear being disliked.

Healthy work relationships require boundaries, agreements, honesty, and trust in others to carry their own weight.

Can Codependency Be Present in Caregiver–Patient Relationships?

Caregiving is fertile ground for codependency, because the roles are already uneven — there is a natural imbalance of power and responsibility and both the caregiver and the patient can interact codependently.

A caregiver may begin to define their entire identity around being needed, pouring so much into the patient that their own needs vanish. Or they may feel overly responsible for the patient's emotional well-being or life choices, neglecting their own needs. Or they may take too much control, leaving the patient little room to make choices. These patterns can lead to resentment, burnout, and/or loss of personal identity.

On the other side, a patient can come to rely so heavily on the caregiver that they don't exercise their own agency. This reliance may reinforce dependency, not just for physical need, but for emotional needs as well, leaving both people in a pool of enmeshment.

Healthy caregiving balances compassion and empathy with boundaries — while allowing agency, dignity, and responsibility.

How Does Codependency Affect Social Interactions?

In social settings, codependency often shows up as people-pleasing. You're scanning the room for approval, adjusting your words, figuring out "who you need to be" to feel accepted and a part of the group. You may be an open book, sharing too much to impress or feel equal to others. Or you may stay on the periphery, looking for just the right conversation to fit in. You may leave a gathering feeling drained, like you were tap-dancing the entire time instead of connecting. Or you may avoid social interactions altogether because the pressure to navigate others' impressions feels overwhelming.

At its heart, codependency in social situations is about losing touch with your authentic self in order to feel safe, accepted, seen, heard, and chosen.

In healthy social interactions, you practice boundaries to listen and remain curious to learn about others. You maintain your own reality, sharing to be known based on your own thoughts and feelings. You can say "no" to invitations without feeling guilt. Ultimately, you can be your authentic self, connecting with others out of freedom and choice.

Chapter **9**

Codependency in Culture and Media

Codependency is frequently portrayed in culture and media — sometimes accurately, sometimes not. This chapter explores how codependency is represented in books, film, TV, and social media, and what it means for how people understand the condition.

How Has the Understanding of Codependency Evolved in Popular Culture?

Codependency evolved from the world of addiction — mostly referring to the spouses of alcoholics and the family members wrapped up in managing someone's drinking. But over time, popular culture has helped widened the lens. Self-help books, talk shows, workshops, and podcasts started exploring how codependency shows up in everyday relationships.

Today, the term gets tossed around more casually, sometimes too casually and without complete understanding, but the upside is that more people are recognizing themselves in these patterns of relating. Codependency is often discussed in terms of trauma and self-care. The chats around codependence have moved into coffee shops, gyms, and walks with friends — they aren't limited to the therapist's office. This shift helps minimize shame, increase understanding, and foster healing.

The challenge is to keep deepening the understanding so people distinguish between healthy interdependence and codependent patterns.

What Role Does Media Play in Shaping Perceptions of Codependency?

Media acts as a double-edged sword in shaping perceptions of codependency. On the one hand, it raises awareness. Books, podcasts, documentaries, and articles give people language for something they feel but can't quite name. Media can show that codependency is rooted in trauma rather than being a weakness or a character flaw. Media can help dispel misunderstandings of what codependency is — and what it isn't.

On the other hand, media can simplify or glamorize codependency, normalizing unhealthy patterns. Media may portray that "true love" requires rescuing the other person, abandoning yourself, or sacrificing everything for love. These are patterns of codependency, not indicators of a healthy, balanced relationship. Media shapes how we see codependency, so accurate portrayals matter.

How Can Accurate Representation of Codependency Help Those Affected?

Clarity is so important for healing. When you see accurate, truthful portrayals of codependency, it helps you understand that it isn't just about being needy, weak, or controlling. You can begin to recognize that codependency is a survival reaction that you learned when you were very young. This recognition helps you feel less shame and opens the door for self-compassion and healing. You aren't "broken." You adapted, out of your intelligence, to survive and figure out ways to get your needs met.

Accurate representations can model healthy behaviors — boundaries, self-care, and the courage to seek help. When you see your story played out truthfully, you realize, "Oh, this isn't just happening to me! I'm not alone!"

What Are the Impacts of Social Media on Codependent Behaviors?

Social media (Facebook, Instagram, and so on) is a hot bed for enabling codependency. Because these platforms are built around feedback — likes, comments, hearts, sad faces, angry faces — external validation can fuel codependent adaptive behaviors such as people-pleasing, seeking approval, and having difficulty setting boundaries. Likes can be addictive and can be a (false) mirror reflecting your value and worth. A lack of likes can be perceived as rejection, disapproval, or abandonment.

On the flip side, social media can also offer resources, awareness, and examples of healing — and some really great recovery quotes! The danger is when the platforms become a substitute for real intimacy and connection. It's easy to lose sight of yourself, to go down rabbit holes, and stay stuck in a familiar survival mode.

TIP

As with all relationships, boundaries are key to a healthy relationship with social media.

How Is Codependency Portrayed in Movies and Television?

Movies and TV shows often include portrayals of codependency without naming it. These portrayals are often in the extreme, romanticized, or seen as comic relief. Maybe it's the overbearing parent who can't let go, or the partner who sacrifices everything to "save" someone spiraling out of control. Sometimes it's a love relationship that shows loving as never letting go, no matter how destructive.

The funny, needy friend, or the controlling spouse — these roles reflect unhealthy dependency and blurred boundaries. What you don't see in these portrayals is a glimpse of the old wounds, the undercurrent of fear and shame that created these adaptive, survival reactions. Movies and TV show the intensity of codependency, but they rarely show the path of healing.

Some examples of movies and TV shows that portray codependency include:

» ***When a Man Loves a Woman:*** This 1994 film starring Meg Ryan and Andy Garcia portrays codependency in the context of addiction. A husband tries to manage his wife's alcoholism, showing how rescuing, though well intentioned, evolves into control and resentment.

» ***Grey's Anatomy:*** The character of Meredith Grey (Ellen Pompeo) highlights people-pleasing, rescuing, and blurred boundaries in several relationships, including with Derek Shepherd (Patrick Dempsey) and Cristina Yang (Sandra Oh).

» ***Jerry Maguire:*** "You complete me." Need we say more?

» ***The White Lotus:*** The character of Tanya McQuoid-Hunt (Jennifer Coolidge) is shown to be desperate for attention, love, and validation.

Are There Any Notable Books That Depict Codependency?

Codependency depicted in memoirs and novels reveals the ways we trade authenticity for connection and abandon ourselves, as well as the powerful impact of codependency on relationships. Here are a few examples:

- » *The Glass Castle* by Jeannette Walls (**Scribner**): A memoir of growing up in a deeply dysfunctional family, where caretaking for unstable parents blurs childhood boundaries.

- » *Love Warrior* by Glennon Doyle (**Flatiron Books**): A memoir of trying to save a marriage and find self-worth through caretaking, and then discovering what real self-love looks like.

- » *The Great Gatsby* by F. Scott Fitzgerald (**Scribner**): Daisy and Gatsby's relationship is based on emotional dependence and the illusion of self as seen through each other's eyes.

- » *Wuthering Heights* by Emily Bronte (**Penguin Classics**): Mutual codependency is portrayed in Catherine and Heathcliff's obsessive relationship.

- » *A Little Life* by Hanya Yanagihara (**Vintage**): Four friends navigate relationships of addiction, success, and brotherly bonds. The novel is about families — those we're born into and those we choose.

Can Music and Art Provide Insights into Codependency?

Art and music can reflect core codependency wounds — the longing for connection, the pain of letting go (abandonment), and the losing of oneself within relationships.

With art, we tell the truth that we don't have words for yet. Perhaps desperate longing for connection is depicted in a painting by merging figures with no space between them (for example, Gustav Klimt's *The Kiss*). Or maybe inner anguish is expressed (as in Edvard Munch's *The Scream*). Or perhaps the self is shown divided (as in Frida Kahlo's *The Two Fridas*).

In music, you hear codependency in love songs that plead, "I can't live without you." You can also hear the pain of self-abandonment and enmeshment in songs such as "I Can't Make You Love Me" by Bonnie Raitt, "Fix You" by Coldplay, and "Every Breath You Take" by The Police.

At the same time, music and art can model healing — finding your voice or celebrating individuality and showing up for yourself. Songs of healing and self-love include the ever classic "I Will Survive" by Gloria Gaynor, "Stronger" by Kelly Clarkson, "Brave" by Sara Bareilles and "You Can Do This Hard Thing" by Carrie Newcomer.

These creative outlets of art and music can be bridges to self-awareness, emotional freedom, and a deep connection to your true self.

Who Are Some Famous Individuals Who Have Spoken about Codependency?

Many public figures have shared openly about codependency in their lives, bringing increased awareness and reducing shame around the issues:

» Singer **Alanis Morissette** has talked about her struggles with people-pleasing and losing herself in relationships. She had a very open, honest interview with Pia Mellody on her podcast, *Conversation with Alanis Morissette* (https://youtu.be/C6JxnskgQBs).

» Actress **Sandra Bullock** has discussed learning to set boundaries after years of over-giving.

» Actor **Hank Azaria** discussed his devastating breakups and his resolve to look inward, address his codependency, and grow in authenticity on an episode of the *Modern Love* podcast (www.nytimes.com/2025/01/15/podcasts/hank-azarias-advice-for-overcoming-codependency.html).

» Researcher and author **Brené Brown** has frequently described her own battles with a need for approval.

When well-known figures name their codependency and share their stories, it normalizes the struggle. It reminds us that codependency is not a weakness, but a reflection of survival skills. We're reminded we're perfectly imperfect. In other words, we are human, and we can learn new ways to love ourselves and others.

3

Recovery and Healing

When you're in the midst of a codependent relationship, you may have a hard time seeing an alternative way forward — but recovery is possible. This part is all about how to recover and heal from codependency, without losing your relationship in the process. It outlines the role of therapy and support groups, how you can experience personal growth as you recover from codependency, and tools and practices you can use on your recovery path, from mindfulness to journaling to goal setting.

Chapter **10**

Beginning Recovery

The good news is that recovery from codependency is possible. This chapter outlines the most effective treatment options, including the forms of therapy shown to help people rebuild healthier patterns of behavior. It also explores the role of support groups and the common challenges that arise along the recovery journey.

What Are the First Steps to Breaking Free from Codependency?

Facing codependency first requires awareness — recognizing the patterns of behavior you've engaged in for years, naming them, and deciding to do something different. When you can see what these patterns have cost you — your voice, your sense of value and worth, your ability to engage in self-care, and your ability to be moderate — the door to change will swing open.

Acting on this awareness is an act of bravery — interrupting your long-practiced patterns feels vulnerable and counterintuitive. This awareness and decision to step forward, with help if necessary, is the first step to a healthier relationship to yourself and others.

How Can Someone Overcome Codependency?

"Overcoming" may not be the ultimate outcome of doing codependency work. Recovery work in codependency isn't about erasing who you are and replacing yourself with a "new you." The codependent wiring is deep-set, a part of your being. But you can learn to override these ingrained pathways with new pathways of behavior. You can learn to hold compassion without losing yourself, to give without abandoning your own needs, to receive without guilt. The process involves healing old wounds, practicing new skills (like boundary setting and communication skills), and building a stronger sense of self. Learning to show up for yourself fully and stay rooted in your inherent value and worth is a process.

Can Therapy Help with Codependency?

Therapy can be a powerful partner to healing codependency. For many people, therapy is the first place to explore family dynamics, notice patterns of behavior in real time, and learn new skills in relating. A therapist can hold a safe space to practice boundaries and experiment with healthier ways of relating. Therapy is also where many people experience being truly seen and heard, without conditions. The therapeutic experience itself begins to heal the wounds that fuel codependency.

What Types of Therapy Are Effective for Treating Codependency?

Several types of therapy can be effective in treating codependency:

» **Family systems work** helps you understand that families, and the people in them, function as one emotional system. By understanding your family story, you understand your own thoughts, feelings, and behaviors.

» **Trauma-informed therapy** helps address the wounds underneath codependency.

» **Attachment-based therapy** focuses on how you learned to connect and bond in relationships.

» **Cognitive behavioral therapy (CBT)** helps you learn to challenge automatic thoughts and reactions that keep you stuck.

» **Eye Movement Desensitization and Reprocessing (EMDR)** helps process traumatic memories and reduce associated distress.

Often an integrated approach works best because codependency isn't just one dimension — it affects identity, emotions, and relationships.

Group therapy can also be beneficial in healing. Codependency thrives in silence and shame, and a group shows you that you're not alone. A group provides a sense of belonging, especially when you hear your stories reflected in others. Groups provide a practice area for boundaries, a place to receive caring feedback, and a place to build healthy connections. Groups are safe spaces to learn that intimacy doesn't have to mean enmeshment and having boundaries doesn't have to mean disconnection.

What Are the Treatment Options for Codependency?

Treatment options for codependency can be varied and layered. Treatment can include individual therapy, group therapy, and support groups like Co-Dependents Anonymous (CoDA). A higher level of care may mean an intensive outpatient program or an inpatient program that specializes in treating codependency. In addition, educational workshops, seminars, retreats, books, podcasts, journaling, and mindfulness practices can help build knowledge and self-awareness.

The best treatment plan is the one that combines insight with practice, awareness, and action.

TIP

How Can Support Groups Aid in Recovery from Codependency?

Support groups, like CoDA, are powerful because they break the isolation and shame associated with codependency. Support groups thrive on *identification* (a group of people with a common problem and a common solution). They're safe spaces where you often hear similar experiences as your own and you witness others navigating and modeling new behaviors of relating. The brain learns best in community, and a support group provides a supportive community to feel seen, heard, and loved.

What Are the Challenges in Breaking Free from Codependency?

Probably the biggest challenge in healing codependency is resistance to change — from yourself and from others. The very nature of creating new habits requires the brain to practice new neural pathways — repeatedly, consistently, over time. The brain's defense system will naturally push back against these new behaviors — doing something different will feel counterintuitive until the new pathways have become more habitual. Codependent patterns are decades old, so change takes time.

Other people may push back and resist your new behaviors as well. When you start setting healthy boundaries, practicing self-care, and using your voice appropriately to state your needs and wants, other people, especially those who may have benefited from your old patterns, may resist.

TIP

You may feel guilt, shame, or fear or think you're being selfish and uncaring. Use your skills anyway! These challenges are opportunities to grow and develop a healthier, more compassionate you.

How Long Does Recovery from Codependency Typically Take?

Recovery from codependency doesn't have a definitive finish line. Early recovery may see shifts in awareness, setting some simple boundaries, practicing some self-care behaviors. If deep trauma is involved, it may take much more time to get to a point where you can experiment with new behaviors.

TIP

You're learning to override a lifetime of behavioral patterns, which were wired in early for your protection. Every pause, every boundary, every act of self-care, every affirmation, and every request for help when needed is a victory and evidence of growth.

You may regress or replay old behaviors when you encounter familiar people, places, or experiences. If and when that happens, your recovery is reflected in how soon you move back into your functional adult state of being.

TIP

Recovery isn't about speed — it's about creating lasting change that allows you to live more freely and more fully.

Chapter **11**

Healing Your Relationship with Yourself

Recovering from codependency isn't just about changing how you relate to others — it's about rebuilding your relationship with yourself. The process can be both challenging and transformative. This chapter explores how codependency can become a catalyst for personal growth, what the stages of that growth look like, and how self-compassion, new coping skills, and persistence lead to lasting change.

How Can Codependency Be a Catalyst for Personal Growth?

As painful as it can be, codependency is often the doorway to deeper healing. When the unknown becomes more attractive than the known, you're brought to a giving-up point where you're more willing to look inward, to examine patterns and behaviors that have not served you, and to discover areas of your life you've neglected or haven't known how to manage. Many people experience this paradox of "surrendering to win," a joy/pain experience that awakens a new way of being — one that's freer, more authentic, and more harmonious.

What Are the Stages of Personal Growth in Overcoming Codependency?

Growth and recovery in codependency work is not a straight path from A to Z with continuous successful upward movement. Growth usually unfolds in stages and can be four steps forward, two steps back. The point is to keep with the commitment toward health, wholeness, and well-being.

The first stage is awareness — naming the patterns and behaviors that are not serving you and the costs associated with them.

The second stage is trying out new behaviors — boundaries, practicing saying no, engaging fully in self-care, and asking for help.

The third stage is integration — these new skills are becoming habits, and you're more easily engaged in your self-care practices without guilt and/or shame, and better able to allow others the dignity and right to their own decisions and behaviors.

In the final stage, you start to notice that your new habits are impacting multiple relationships, and you begin to trust more and more our capacity to show up for yourself, living more in a state of freedom, compassion, and harmony.

What Personal Strengths Are Often Developed through Codependency Work?

Doing codependency work is not for the faint of heart! The work asks you to bring your whole self into your relationship with yourself and your relationships with others. This work fosters resilience, empathy, courage, trust, patience, and authenticity. The work adds critical skills to your life — setting healthy boundaries, using your voice to respectfully communicate your needs and wants, listening with curiosity, and engaging fully in your self-care. Perhaps the greatest strength developed in this work is knowing you have inherent value and worth and that your worth is not dependent on another person's behavior, approval, or acknowledgment.

What Role Does Self-Compassion Play in Recovery from Codependency?

Self-compassion is what allows you to hold two truths at one time: You're human, fallible, and error-prone, and *at the same time,* you're precious, worthwhile, and enough. Self-compassion softens your inner critic and allows you to treat yourself as you would others — with patience, care, and forgiveness. It helps you not to judge yourself too harshly when you repeat old patterns. With self-compassion, you can remind yourself, "Right, I burp, I fart, I mess up, and I can be a pain sometimes. None of this define my worth. It just means I'm human and still learning. Onward."

How Can I Develop Healthier Coping Mechanisms to Replace Codependent Patterns?

Replacing codependent patterns is a process, not an event. These patterns have been with you since you were very young. They helped protect you and helped you get your needs met. Identifying those early needs is part of the first steps of awareness. If you over give to feel valued, you can practice affirming yourself instead. If you numb out on social media, you can journal or take a walk to ground yourself. Healthier coping mechanisms often include mindfulness, creativity, movement, or reaching out to safe support. The key is practicing these new skills that bring you back to yourself (rather than pull you away) repeatedly, consistently, and over time. Practice makes permanent, not perfect.

How Do I Handle Setbacks in Codependency Recovery?

You handle setbacks with self-compassion, kindness, and forgiveness. Setbacks are a part of the process. The struggle, the setback, the hurdle — each is a teacher to bring your awareness to what you're still learning. Setbacks are opportunities to pause, reflect, and choose what to do differently next time, without shame and self-criticism. Progress in recovery is measured over time — remember to look at the arc of your recovery, the big picture, to note how you've grown and how you show up for yourself differently now.

What Are the Long-Term Benefits of Addressing and Overcoming Codependency?

The benefits of addressing codependency are life-changing. You gain the ability to show up fully for yourself and to live from choice rather than from fear, duty, or obligation. Recovery creates harmony within yourself, resulting in more harmonious relationships with others. You can give and receive without losing yourself and more readily detach from outcomes, releasing the need for others to feel, think, or behave a certain way for you to feel valued and/or secure. You develop a sense of self-worth that is intrinsic, not dependent on anyone else's approval, resulting in a connection to self and others that is healthier, richer, and more sustainable.

Chapter **12**

Tools and Practices for Recovery

Recovery from codependency is a process. Although therapy and support groups are crucial, you can practice skills and use tools that help you notice old patterns, experiment with new behaviors, and measure your progress over time. This chapter includes exercises that can help support your journey toward autonomy, balance, and self-trust.

Are There Any Specific Exercises to Help with Codependency?

Exercises are powerful practices to help create new responses to your relationship with yourself and your relationships with others. Practice just *pausing* — taking a moment to notice how your body is feeling, to notice the thoughts you're having, and to name any feelings you're experiencing. This is an important exercise to help you discern old behaviors from new.

Practice writing and speaking *affirmations* (for example, "I deserve to have and speak my own thoughts, feelings, and behaviors" or "I am capable of having healthy boundaries and allowing others to have theirs").

Notice each day when you feel the urgency to say "yes" but really mean "no" and then actually say "no" instead. That's a powerful boundary-building practice. So is practicing the healthy communication skill of listening with curiosity and speaking to be known.

These exercises may seem small or insignificant at first, but with consistent repetition, they create new neural pathways that override the old reactions so you can honor your goal of being less codependent and better at showing up for yourself in a healthy way.

How Can Mindfulness Practices Aid in Addressing Codependent Behaviors?

Mindfulness slows down the autopilot reactions that drive codependency. Mindfulness invites you to pause and notice your body sensations and your feelings, and be able to ask, "What's happening inside me?," "How am I feeling about this?," and "What's w to take care of and what's the other person's work?"

Mindfulness creates the space to respond with *choice* rather than reactivity, obligation, or the sense that you "have to" or "should." Over time, mindfulness becomes a grounding practice that helps you hold compassion for yourself and others without losing yourself and helps you remain centered and present.

What Are the Benefits of Journaling in the Context of Codependency Recovery?

Journaling moves your inner voice and feelings to paper. It gives you a way to see patterns — situations where you abandon yourself and have unskilled boundaries or feelings you may ignore. In addition, journaling shows evidence of your growth. Writing it down gives you evidence that you can change, shows your progress, and helps you feel less shame because you're putting truth to paper and no longer hiding.

How Can Setting Personal Goals Aid in Overcoming Codependency?

Setting personal goals helps provide structure, motivation, and a road map for the change you desire. Goals help you foster accountability — reminding you that your recovery is your work and doesn't come from external sources.

Your goals don't have to be huge or a certain number. A goal can be as simple as "I will practice saying 'no' at least once a week" or "I will engage in three acts of self-care each week." When you meet your goals, you build trust in yourself, which offsets the self-doubt that fuels codependency. And when you don't meet your goals, you can remember that you're human, not perfect, and you can reassess and try again.

How Can I Build a Support Network to Aid in My Personal Growth?

Surrounding yourself with people who honor your healing, who want you to succeed, who respect your boundaries, and who celebrate your progress is an important part of codependency recovery. A support network may include trusted friends, a therapist, mentors, and/or a recovery group.

Sometimes you may need to step back from relationships that reinforce old behaviors, sabotage your progress, or don't provide compassionate support for your desire for change. A strong support group mirrors how you want to be and provides safe and gentle feedback when you struggle.

How Can I Track My Progress in Navigating Codependency?

Progress in codependency recovery can show up in subtle ways. Tracking progress may include journaling — noting situations where you responded differently than you used to. Maybe you pause more often, ask for help without guilt, or say no without shaming yourself. Maybe you notice more how your body feels.

Another way to track progress is with an accountability partner, perhaps a 12-step program sponsor or a trusted friend. When you hear others remark that they see changes in you, that gives you data that change is indeed possible and that you're doing it!

Progress isn't an event — it's a process. Keep looking, and you'll see the signs of change. And when you can't, don't give up, keep stepping forward — you'll see signs of change as you continue to practice, practice, practice.

How Can I Rebuild My Self-Esteem in Recovery?

Healthy self-esteem is a relationship with your authentic state of being — a connection with your inherent value and worth. Codependency sets you up to fluctuate between a sense of "less than" and a sense of "better than." In codependency, your concept of self-esteem is formed and defined through the affirmations of others or by comparing yourself to others. Codependency is "other esteeming" rather than "self-esteeming." Rebuilding your self-esteem involves affirming that your value and worth are inherent, not dependent on external sources. You practice owning this inherent value and worth even when you witness yourself being human and imperfect.

Self-esteem grows when you notice your needs and honor them, when you witness yourself practicing healthy boundaries, and when you can pause to catch yourself being self-critical and gently replace it with self-compassion. Surrounding yourself with people who affirm your value and worth in a healthy way is helpful, but ultimately developing your self-esteem is an inside job. Each act of self-love, self-compassion, and forgiveness, no matter how small, is a building block for strong self-esteem.

How Can I Foster Healthy Boundaries?

Healthy boundaries are a system of protecting yourself from being a victim and containing yourself so that you aren't offensive to others. Damaged boundaries — boundaries in code-pendent patterns — fluctuate on a continuum of "too little" boundary (not enough protection and/or not enough containment) and "too much" boundary (walled off from others and/or walled off from self). Fostering healthy bound-aries first involves awareness — tuning into your own thoughts, feelings, behaviors — and being aware what feels okay for you and what doesn't. When you can name what's okay and what isn't, then you practice communicating these limits with respect, kindness, and confidence to oth-ers. Over time, you become less fearful setting boundaries and set them as an act of love for yourself and for others.

How Can I Create a Healthy Sense of Reality?

A healthy sense of reality gives meaning to what you see, hear, smell, and taste. Reality also reflects your thoughts about an experience, your emotions that you feel about an experience, and your behavior in response to the experience. Codependency distorts your reality because you're tuned into others' needs and feelings and lose sight of your own. In codependency, you have a difficult time separating your truth from other people's stories — often creating a continuum of being bad/rebellious or good/perfect in order to get your needs met. Creating a healthy reality starts with asking yourself: "What do *I* feel?, What do *I* need? What do *I* want to do? What is in *my* best interest?" Therapy, journaling, mindfulness, and support groups all help you learn to ground yourself in your own reality.

What Role Does Self-Care Play in Overcoming Codependency?

Self-care is both the practice and the symbol of recovery. Self-care is about how we show up to care for your needs and wants — including physical, financial, mental, emotional, social, and medical needs. Codependency creates extremes of "too dependent" at one end and "needless/wantless" at the other. Codependent patterns may look like over-giving, people-pleasing, asking others to do for you what you need to be doing for yourself. Or, you may try to be Superman or Wonder Woman and appear not to need any help because you believe that asking for help is a sign of weakness.

Codependency tells you that self-care is self-ish and indulgent. But in recovery, self-care is not indulgent — it's a healthy, appropriate act of showing up fully for yourself. It can look like rest, movement, therapy, healthy nutrition, bill paying, spiritual practices, saying "no" when you're drained, saying "yes" when you really want to experience an event. Self-care says, "I take care of my needs and wants, and when I can't, I ask for help from an appropriate resource."

How Can I Develop a More Moderate Lifestyle in Recovery?

"Moderation in all things" is the healthy goal in this core practice. Codependency creates the extremes of too little maturity/out of control (which results in chaos) and too much maturity/too much control (which results in lack of connection). Moderation comes from learning to have healthy boundaries so we can experience spontaneity and being real and connected with life in the moment. It means being relational without being offensive. Moderation is freedom. You're no longer living in survival mode, but in harmony. You're creating moderate rhythms of work, play, rest, and connection.

4

Building and Sustaining Healthy Relationships

This part explains what healthy relationships look like and how you can establish healthy relationships with your family and your romantic partner. It also offers resources for support on the road ahead.

Chapter **13**

Family and Partnership Dynamics

Your family of origin shapes the patterns that lead to codependency, but healing doesn't mean severing ties. Recovery is about understanding how you show up in relationships and learning to engage in healthy, balanced ways. This chapter explores what healthy relationships look like, strategies for setting boundaries with family, and more.

Can Codependency Be Resolved without Ending Relationships?

Codependency isn't about the relationship itself, but about how you show up inside the relationship. As one person in the relationship begins to practice new behaviors — having healthier boundaries, speaking with honesty, honoring their own needs, engaging in self-care — the dynamic with others will naturally shift. As one person changes, others may change in tandem — especially if they're committed to their own work.

Sometimes other people resist the changes in the family member doing their recovery work — it may feel threatening, unfamiliar, or out of balance. In these cases, the one learning the skills, is the one who does the work — meaning healing can happen even if others aren't involved in their own work.

You don't have to walk away, but you get to determine how to take care of yourself while choosing to be in relationship with others who may or may not be doing their own work.

TIP

Others don't have to change in order for you to get better.

What Are the Signs of Healthy, Functional Relationships?

A primary sign of a healthy, functional, secure relationship (non-codependent) is the evidence of mutual investment. Shared investment emotionally, mentally, physically, sexually, financially — not necessarily 50/50, but with agreement as to how each person is contributing to the success of the relationship.

People in healthy relationships have and respect boundaries and can communicate honestly without fear of being judged, discounted, or abandoned. Each person takes responsibility for their own feelings, thoughts, and actions. Conflict is courageously met with steps toward repair. Care flows both ways — without overgiving, controlling, or being overly dependent. You feel safe being vulnerable without fear of losing your identity.

Healthy relationships feel spacious — with room to be yourself, to grow without fear, and with the knowledge that others want your well-being.

How Can I Establish Boundaries in My Family?

Boundaries in families can feel very challenging because everyone has had the same roles and patterns of relating for years. The first step to establish boundaries is awareness — knowing what's negotiable and nonnegotiable, what you want and don't want, what's yours and what isn't.

Next, you learn to share and communicate your boundaries with love and respect (not control, intimidation, or ultimatums). Detaching (with love) is another practice — allowing others the dignity and right to have their own thoughts, feelings, and reactions to your boundaries.

Family members may push back, question you, or be critical in some way that indicates they're having a reaction to your new patterns. Let them! *Remember:* Boundaries are about protecting and containing yourself — your own integrity, energy, and well-being. Without help, this can be a difficult journey for family members.

TIP

Here are some boundary statements to practice:

>> I can't do that, but I can listen or help you find someone who can.

>> I can't attend, but I appreciate the invite.

>> I'm uncomfortable with what you just said/ did. In the future I'd prefer. . . .

>> I'm happy to go to the event, and I'll be taking my own car.

>> That sounds difficult. What have you thought about doing?

>> Thank you. (without explanation)

>> No. (without explanation)

How Can Communication Skills Help Foster Family Relationships?

Clear, honest, compassionate communication is like oxygen to families — keeping relationships alive, flowing, and growing. Healthy communication reminds each person that they're responsible for their own thoughts, feelings, and behaviors, as well as the impact those thoughts, feelings, and behaviors have on others. Communication is a skill that can be learned and improved upon. Learning to share or speak in order to be known is quite different from sharing to control, blame, defend, or elicit a specific outcome from others. Similarly, listening to learn (with curiosity) is quite different from listening to form a defense.

Practice skills include using "I" statements, actively listening, keeping shared agreements, and pausing before responding (in order to honor boundaries). Many families need help learning these skills, but when new patterns start to become more habitual, love, respect, and compassion build, fostering close and healthy families.

How Can Partners Work Together to Avoid Codependent Patterns?

Working together in a couple in order to minimize codependent patterns involves practicing healthy boundaries, talking openly about fears and needs, and establishing clear agreements. Partners can practice checking in regularly to assess the harmony of the relationship. You and your partner can take stock of the relationship, asking "How are we doing?" emotionally, physically, sexually, mentally, and financially.

TIP

Actively showing your partner you have their back, watching for ways to contribute to their emotional bank account, and spending intentional time with your partner are all ways partners can anchor a healthy relationship and minimize the old patterns.

How Can I Maintain Independence in a Relationship?

Independence in a relationship isn't about distance — it's about staying grounded in your own state of being while in connection with another person. "What would I be doing if I weren't in a relationship?" is a great question to ask if you get stuck maintaining your individuality within a relationship. Would you be going out with friends? Taking a ukelele class? Going to see that Broadway show you've heard about? Keeping these individual interests alive will help you develop personal boundaries and the ability to own your reality within a relationship. Individually watching for old patterns of survival — saying yes when you want to say no, avoiding spending time with friends because you think your partner would disapprove, or not using your voice to avoid conflict — is an important practice when building healthy partnerships.

TIP

Independence is the freedom to be you — to bring your whole self to the relationship without needing to shrink or merge in order to keep the relationship safe.

What Is the Role of Mutual Respect in Healthy Relationships?

Respect is the minimum of being loving. Respect in a relationship sounds like, "I honor your boundaries, just as I expect you to honor mine" or, "I honor your thoughts and feelings, even if they're different from mine." Respect is the foundation that keeps power balanced — neither person is the parent and neither is the child. Respect makes space for equality and vulnerability, allowing intimacy to deepen. Respect keeps love from shifting into caretaking or control. With respect, relationships feel like mutually invested partnerships.

What Are Some Important Communication Skills for Partnerships?

Effective communication means learning to speak or share in order to be known by another and to listen with curiosity in order to learn about the other person. Sharing to be known requires a boundary of containment to honestly share how you're making yourself feel or think about an event. You do this without blame, manipulation, and/or attachment to an outcome. Listening to learn requires a boundary of protection — the ability to hold the other person at arm's length (figuratively) in order to listen to them with curiosity while they're sharing. You try to do this without rushing to fix, defend, justify, minimize, or explain. (This may sound foreign to you, but remember that it's a skill to be learned — it won't come naturally because of your years of wired survival responses.)

Using "I" statements, slowing down your responses, and checking for understanding are practices that help you stay connected in the moment. Reflecting *affect* (the other person's feeling) before offering information is another useful practice (for example, "That sounds awful," "I can tell you're really upset about that," "Boy, that's difficult").

TIP

Healthy communication in partnerships isn't so much about using "perfect" words; it's more about staying present, open, and boundaried, even when the conversation is uncomfortable.

How Can Trust Be Built in a Relationship?

To be trusted, you need to be trustworthy. Easier said than done, of course. Trust grows when you witness consistent behaviors over time. Practicing integrity in a relationship builds trust. This looks like being where you say you're going to be, at the time you say you'll be there, with the people you say you'll be with. Trust builds when you own your mistakes, make amends, and show your changed behaviors rather than just talk about what you're going to do.

Trust also grows when you risk being vulnerable — sharing fears, hopes, sadnesses — and when you can meet that vulnerability from others with care and compassion instead of dismissal or judgment. Building trust is not the result of one grand gesture. It's the by-product of a thousand little actions that say, "I'm here for you. You can count on me, and I'm counting on you." Trust is a skilled decision and an important practice in compassionate self-care.

What Are the Benefits of Mutual Investment in Relationships?

Mutual investment includes emotional, mental, physical, sexual, and financial presence and care. It doesn't have to be 50/50, but both partners need to be making an intentional effort.

Mutual investment in relationships is the foundation for a safe, supportive, and secure space. Mutual investment lowers stress and emotional exhaustion and replaces them with shared responsibility and mutual support. It decreases fears of abandonment, decreases compulsive controlling behaviors, and decreases resentments. It increases a cycle of interdependence, replacing old patterns of rescuing and over-involvement. It also enhances communication and problem-solving skills, which helps partners move from conflict into repair more quickly and smoothly. Mutual investment reminds both partners that the work of the relationship doesn't fall on one person's shoulders. Both partners are showing up, leaning in, and actively taking part. This mutual energy in the relationship builds resilience, respect, and a sense of shared responsibility — reminding each partner that they aren't alone, but hand in hand on a shared journey.

What Role Does Empathy Play in Codependent Relationships?

Empathy (understanding and sharing the feelings of another person) can be a double-edged sword in relationships when one or both partners is in recovery from their codependent patterns. On the one hand, empathy creates a deep emotional connection and allows you to relate to another person's experience. On the other hand, in your codependency patterns, empathy can get distorted into over-responsibility, rescuing, or believing it's your job to fix the other person. In codependency, empathy says, "I can't be okay when you're not okay" or, "I need to help get your boat steady, so I can feel steady." Healthy empathy says, "I see you, I hear you, I understand you're struggling, and I allow you the dignity and right to engage in your self-care." Learning this difference is what turns empathy from a trap to a gift.

Chapter **14**

Maintaining Recovery and Support

Recovery from codependency is a lifelong process, and numerous resources are available to help you along the way. In this chapter, I steer you toward resources that can help you on the journey ahead.

What Resources Are Available for Those Struggling with Codependency?

A wide range of resources is available for those struggling with codependency. Many treatment facilities now offer specialized treatment for codependency. Therapy — both individual and group — is widely available, and it's a core support for learning new patterns of relating to yourself and others. Support groups offer ongoing and foundational support, as well as peer connections. Podcasts, seminars, retreats, workshops, books, online communities — all provide support, deeper understanding, and models of new behavior patterns.

TIP

When choosing resources, look for those that help you shift from old survival patterns to new patterns of healthy boundaries, self-care, and moderation. Choose resources that encourage inner work. Look for safe connections that provide compassionate support.

What Are the Best Support Groups for Codependency?

Co-Dependents Anonymous (CoDA) is the most well-known support group for codependency. It's modeled after the 12-step tradition of Alcoholics Anonymous. Al-Anon can also be helpful, especially if your partner is addicted to alcohol. Some people find that Adult Children of Alcoholics addresses many issues if they've grown up in a family with addictions. Some treatment centers may offer public support groups and, of course, many therapists facilitate local or online support groups tailored to codependency.

TIP

The "best" group is the one where you feel safe, seen, and supported. Sometimes it takes visiting a few groups over a significant period of time before you find your fit.

Are There Helpful Books on Codependency?

Over the past years, many more books have been published to help bring codependency into everyday conversation. Here are some I recommend:

» *Codependent No More* by Melody Beattie (Hazelden) is foundational for many people, as are her *The Language of Letting Go* daily meditation books. *The New Codependency* (Simon & Schuster) is her updated version, providing new insights and strategies for readers.

» *Facing Codependence* by Pia Mellody (Harper & Row) goes deeper into developmental roots and provides in-depth understanding of the five core symptoms of codependence. Mellody's book *The Intimacy Factor*

(HarperOne) explores the impact of codependency on relationships and provides strategies for developing intimacy and true love in relationships.

» *Codependency For Dummies* by Darlene Lancer (Wiley) is a comprehensive guide on codependency and gives practical advice and exercises for recovery.

» *Boundaries: When to Say Yes, How to Say No to Take Control of Your Life* by Henry Cloud and John Townsend (Zondervan) doesn't spend too much time on codependency but does give readers a reference for assessing boundaries (or lack thereof) and how to build and communicate healthy boundaries.

» *Women Who Love Too Much* by Robin Norwood (Tarcher) explores the patterns of women who become overly involved in their relationships and provides strategies for healthier relationships. It includes a great description of the "codependent dance."

» *Personal Boundaries For Dummies* by Victoria Priya (Wiley) is a great book to navigate the challenging boundaries present in relationships and specific guidance on how to practice healthier boundaries.

» *Growing Yourself Back Up* by John Lee (Harmony) explains how seemingly uncontrollable feelings are directly related to childhood experiences and provides methods and exercises for emotional regulation.

» *Gifts from a Challenging Childhood* by Jan Bergstrom (Mountain Stream Publishing) breaks down the core areas of codependency and how they developed in childhood, with specific examples and healing exercise to create a more functional self.

There are also many books that integrate trauma healing, attachment theory, or mindfulness. Though books aren't the whole journey, they can give language to what you're living, and that often sparks the first steps of healing.

Can Podcasts, Seminars, Workshops, Retreats, or Education Be Helpful?

Additional resources, like podcasts, workshops, seminars, retreats, and educational programs give you reminders that you aren't alone, that there is hope, and that others have learned new patterns of relating and you can, too. Podcasts often have guests who relate their stories honestly and in a way that you readily identify with. Workshops, seminars, and retreats can immerse you in a different way of relating, sharing, and learning, which is often life-changing. Education — whether through classes, trainings, or books — helps you understand why you do what you do, which reduces shame. These tools can't replace deep inner therapeutic work, but they can strengthen, support, and sustain it.

Are There Specific Skills for Healthy Social Media Interactions?

Social media can either reinforce codependent patterns and tendencies or be a place to practice healthy boundaries and new patterns of relating. Healthy social media skills include pausing before you respond, noticing if you're seeking validation, and limiting comparisons. A good self-check may be to ask yourself, "Am I posting to express myself, or to get approval and/or validation?" If you're checking and rechecking your post for comments and likes, you have your answer.

TIP

A good boundary practice is curating your feed so it supports rather than drains you. In short, using social media with awareness and limits can turn it from a trigger into a tool for connection.

Are There Any Mobile Apps for Managing Codependent Patterns?

Many apps are designed for emotional health, boundary-setting, and recovery work, many of which can support codependency healing. Meditation and mindfulness tools like Insight Timer, Calm, and Headspace, can help you learn to stay connected to yourself. I Am is a daily affirmation app with exercise and reminders. Moodfit is another app that's helpful for tracking moods, feelings, sleep, and nutrition. Journaling and gratitude apps also can be very helpful. Some recovery communities, including CoDA, have meeting locators and digital tools.

TIP

The app itself isn't the cure — but if it helps you pause, reflect, or connect to support instead of defaulting to old patterns, it's serving its purpose.

How Can I Find a Therapist Specializing in Codependency?

Seeking therapy is an act of self-love. Start by looking for therapists who name codependency, boundaries, family systems, family-of-origin issues, or trauma recovery in their specialties. Many therapists who work with addictions or relationship issues are able to work with codependency as well.

TIP

Online directories like Psychology Today (www.psychologytoday.com/us/therapists), TherapyDen (www.therapyden.com), or local counseling associations can be helpful.

Do you know someone already in therapy for their codependency? Ask about their therapist. You can also contact treatment centers that specialize in codependency treatment and ask for trained therapists in your area.

Most important, when you meet with a therapist, notice how you feel: Do you feel seen, heard, safe, and respected? That connection matters as much as their training.

What Questions Should I Ask My Therapist about Codependency?

Because the connection with a therapist is as important as their knowledge and skill set, here are some questions you may want to ask when you make contact with a therapist:

>> Do you have specific knowledge and training in codependency?

>> How do you approach codependency in your practice?

>> What is your experience with family-of-origin issues, childhood trauma, and attachment theory?

>> How do you address and teach boundaries, self-care practices, communication skills, and living in moderation and truth?

>> How do we measure progress together?

These questions may help provide clarity about the therapist's practice, skills, and style. You're also noticing if the therapist feels human and relatable — an arrogant therapist won't help you.

TIP

You're a consumer of a specific service. Ask questions, be curious and observant, and check in with your gut to see if it feels like a safe and supportive therapeutic partnership.

How Can Family Members Support Someone Struggling with Codependency?

The paradox of family support is that the best way to help is often by following the three gets: Get off their back, get out of their way, and get on with your life. This advice sounds harsh until family members educate themselves in what codependency is, how it shows up, and their role in enabling the codependent patterns.

Detaching with love is not abandoning your loved one. It's allowing them the dignity and right to their own recovery process, trusting they can walk their own path, and trusting that their resources of support (their therapist, treatment team, and support group) can help them better than a family member can.

TIP

Instead of rescuing, directing, controlling, or shaming, family members can show support by encouraging connections to resources, respecting boundaries, and celebrating small steps. Family members usually need help practicing these new behaviors. Seek it. You deserve support and care as much as your loved one.

What Role Do Friends Play in the Recovery from Codependence?

The suggestions for support from friends is very similar to the suggestions for family members (see the preceding section). Friends who can detach with love, support healthy self-care, and encourage maintaining connections with appropriate support systems will be most helpful to the recovering codependent. Friendships can be healthy places to practice honesty, to set boundaries, and to receive care and support without judgment or shame. Good friends can act as a mirror — reflecting back your value and worth, your progress, and any concerns when you may be slipping into old patterns.

TIP

Being discerning with your friendships is important. Surround yourself with those friends who can respect your journey. Have more boundaries with those who activate you into your old patterns of over giving, rescuing, people-pleasing, or self-neglect.

How Can I Stay Motivated during Codependency Recovery?

Nobody can save you from your history. Staying motivated with your work will ebb and flow — that's natural. Remember it's a process, not an event. As you continue to practice new patterns of responding to your world, it'll be easier to move back into a functional, secure space when your motivation dips.

You can't always be "on" — that's okay. Give yourself grace and compassion when you notice yourself wavering, wanting to quit, or thinking you're never going to get better. When you notice these feelings, reach into your toolbox and pick a tool. If you need help doing that, make a call or reach out. Ask someone to remind you of your inherent value and worth, of your progress. Choose someone who will cheer you on and give you permission to be human.

Keep a journal, check in with your support group, go to a meeting, listen to a podcast, repeat your affirmations out loud, dance! You will not *extinguish* your original survival responses, but as you practice healthier responses more and more often over time, you will override the first protective wiring, living more often in your new patterns than your old patterns. You'll breathe easier in relationships, trust yourself more, and know your worth isn't tied to fixing or pleasing others.

TIP

Recovery isn't about perfection — there is no such thing. It's about living more in *skilled* choices than *unskilled* choices. It's less about losing the old you and more about reclaiming the self you've always been.

Index

Dedication

I dedicate this book to Pia Mellody — my teacher, mentor, and role model. Her work, her friendship, and her support brought such light to my journey when I needed it most. Her voice continues to guide my work and my daily experience of being a human.

I owe deep thanks and gratitude to my family, my Posse, my friends, and my colleagues whose ongoing love and support brings me such joy. You all make my heart sing.

And finally I thank my clients, whose courage to entrust their journey with me is such a privilege and honor.

—Cynthia Schiebel

Publisher's Acknowledgments

Senior Managing Editor:
Kristie Pyles

Associate Editor:
Elizabeth Stilwell

Editor: Elizabeth Kuball

Production Editor:
Tamilmani Varadharaj

Cover Design and Image:
Wiley

Special Help:
Carmen Krikorian

About the Authors

Cynthia Schiebel, MEd, LPC, LCDC: Cynthia Schiebel is a Licensed Professional Counselor and a Licensed Chemical Dependency Counselor. She lives and works in Austin, Texas, where she has an active private counseling practice. Cynthia's many years of training with Pia Mellody inform her therapeutic work in codependence, addictions, relationship health, and spiritual development. She has also trained and studied with Stan Tatkin (Level II PACT), Terry Real, Richard Schwartz (IFS Informed), and Thomas Huble. Also a board-certified coach, Cynthia enjoys working with individuals and teams exploring relationship skills, life transitions, and authentic living. Prior to private practice, Cynthia served 28 years in public education as a speech pathologist, school counselor, and administrator. Her years coordinating Title IV, Safe and Drug-Free Schools and Communities programs influenced her deep interest in childhood trauma, the impact of family relationships, and the hope and joy of recovery processes. In addition to her vocation, Cynthia's avocations include acting, ushering at local theaters, and travel adventures.

Darlene Lancer, JD, LMFT: Darlene Lancer is a licensed marriage and family therapist and an expert and author on relationships and codependency. She has counseled individuals and couples for more than 30 years and coaches internationally.